Emilola Shyllon

HOPE, MY SOUL'S ANCHOR.
Copyright © 2017 by Emilola Shyllon

All rights reserved. This book or any portion thereof may not be reproduced or used in any manner whatsoever without the express permission of the publisher except for the use of brief quotations in a book review.

Scripture taken from The Message. Copyright © 1993, 1994, 1995, 1996, 2000, 2001, 2002. Used by permission of NavPress Publishing Group.

Scripture taken from the New King James Version®. Copyright © 1982 by Thomas Nelson. Used by permission. All rights reserved.

Scripture quotations marked (NASB) are taken from the New American Standard Bible®, Copyright © 1960, 1962, 1963, 1968, 1971, 1972, 1973,1975, 1977, 1995 by The Lockman Foundation Used by permission. (www.Lockman.org)

Scripture quotations marked (AMP) are taken from the Amplified® Bible, Copyright © 1954, 1958, 1962, 1964, 1965, 1987 by The Lockman Foundation. Used by permission. (www.Lockman.org)

Scripture quotations marked (NLT) are taken from the Holy Bible, New Living Translation, copyright © 1996, 2004, 2007 by Tyndale House Foundation. Used by permission of Tyndale House Publishers, Inc., Carol Stream, Illinois 60188. All rights reserved.

THE HOLY BIBLE, NEW INTERNATIONAL VERSION®, NIV® Copyright © 1973, 1978, 1984, 2011 by Biblica, Inc.® Used by permission. All rights reserved worldwide.

Scripture quotations marked (ESV) are from The Holy Bible, English Standard Version® (ESV®), Copyright © 2001 by Crossway, a publishing ministry of Good News Publishers. Used by permission. All rights reserved.

Scripture quotations marked KJV are taken from the King James Bible.

DAY 18 - "Trading My Sorrows (Yes Lord)" by Darrell Evans, Copyright ©1998, 2002.

ISBN 978-1-9997689-0-4

Cover Photo by Shutterstock.com/ Xtuv Photography
Cover design and book layout by Emanations

First Printing, 2017.
Printed in the United Kingdom

TESTIMONIALS

I have had the joy of knowing Emi for several years as part of Hope Church, and since the publication of her first devotional, I have eagerly awaited the next! Her obvious passion for God is infectious and her desire and ability to hear from Him spills out in blessing others. The wisdom she shares in this devotional comes from personal experience as she has sought God in the circumstances of her own life.

The time and effort that goes on behind the scenes to produce a work such as this is immense, and I know her joy will be complete if it serves to bless the reader. "The proof of the pudding is in the eating", as the saying goes, and as you feast on this devotional, you will without doubt find nourishment for your soul. Enjoy!

Marion Palmer
Author - One more step

When Lola asked me to review her manuscript, I took it as just another script I had to go through but as I read .... there was no choice but to pause at the end of each page. All that kept resounding in my heart was a theme of Hope... Hope, to be able to navigate these really murky waters of daily living. Hope ... to breathe again, hope to see light coming from darkness. Well! Lola, now you know the truth behind why it took me longer than planned to edit... I finally confess. When all of life is bleak and moments are grey, Hope is the anchor that helps me stay...
It is a gift to be able to write but it is a blessing to truly inspire.... "Hope, my soul's anchor"...
Lola, I am truly inspired...

Oyin Idowu

Testimonials

Having gone through a really rough patch in my personal life, I know more than most how hard it can be to 'climb' back out of a dark place emotionally and spiritually. When I read this book, I wished it existed during my 'trying' phase as all I needed then, I can now see in the pages of this book.

This devotional will work and walk with you daily to bring much needed encouragement for your soul through easy-to read text and short Scriptures to give you a boost and anchor you in the midst of life's choppy waters that threaten to pull you down.

Funmi Onamusi
Author, Help! I am a Mum

The title of this new devotional reminds me of one of my favourite hymns: Will Your Anchor Hold In The Storms of Life? Singing it always ministers hope to my soul. As I went through the manuscript, I discovered that each day's capsule of 'Hope, My Soul's Anchor' is spiritually medicinal and gave me a spiritual uplift. I'm not surprised that the last one year revealed Mrs Emilola Shyllon's hidden talent as a budding scriptural author, the first of which was the highly acclaimed 31-day Christian devotional titled 'Springs of Living Water'. It is with the above in mind that I can confidently assert my personal gratefulness to God for being privileged to have Emilola as a wonderful spiritual daughter whose latest devotional will undoubtedly minister to the souls of many. Be blessed.

Pastor Solomon Oke
The Redeemed Christian Church of God,
Rabboni Parish, Stevenage

CONTENTS

Acknowledgements 7

Foreword 9

Introduction 11

Dedication 15

DAY 1   Don't Give Up 16

DAY 2   Dealing With Giants 18

DAY 3   Not Without A Struggle 20

DAY 4   "Do It Afraid" 22

DAY 5   Your Focus 24

DAY 6   A Precious Ointment, A Costly Worship 26

DAY 7   I Wonder 28

DAY 8   Beyond Redemption? 30

DAY 9   "404 Not Found Error" 32

DAY 10 Counted Joy, Considered Joy 34

DAY 11 Seven Times Hotter (1) 36

DAY 12 Seven Times Hotter (2) 38

DAY 13 My Scars, Your Proof 40

DAY 14 He Calls You By Name 42

DAY 15 How To Dress For Victory (1) 44

DAY 16 How To Dress For Victory (2) 46

DAY 17 The Lord's Battle 48

DAY 18 Trading Places 50

DAY 19 Heart Conditions 52

Contents

DAY 20	Lessons From Lazarus	54
DAY 21	Transition	56
DAY 22	It Runs In The Family	58
DAY 23	A Reminder	60
DAY 24	"E For Effort Not Excuses"	62
DAY 25	Your Welfare Package	64
DAY 26	Made To Prosper, Made For More	66
DAY 27	Prison Mates	68
DAY 28	Lessons From A Boat (1)	70
DAY 29	Lessons From A Boat (2)	72
DAY 30	The Main Thing	74
DAY 31	My Life, A Contradiction	76
Sinner's Prayer		78

ACKNOWLEDGEMENTS

To my Father, and my God, my Deliverer, the Glory and the Lifter of my head. The One whose comfort reaches places no other comfort will do – I praise and I thank you.

No project is ever completed without the help of many people. It would be impossible to list everyone who has impacted me in the writing of this devotional. However, special thanks go out to the following people:

To my best friend and husband, Olayemi for the practical help that made this work possible. I still appreciate you for the space you give to be all of me and more reasons besides.

To my earthly father, Jide, for countless hours of prayers, encouragement, timely Scriptural text messages and wise counsel.

To my siblings Faramade and Adetola Oyenuga. You guys are the best brothers a girl could wish for! Thanks for your hearty responses in time of need. Tola - thanks for capturing such brilliant photographs. Yetunde Olukolu - our God still answers prayers, massively! Thank you for years of 24-carat friendship and prayer times across time zones.

To all my friends and wider family, impossible to name you all – thank you for the support you give.

To Pastor Oke, for pastoral care without equal. Your investment of time and prayers is difficult to quantify. My heartfelt appreciation to you and your wife for laying open your hearts and home to us.

Acknowledgements

To Marion Palmer, Funmi Onamusi and Oyinkan Idowu, for your unalloyed friendship, super timely encouragement, and your painstaking efforts at reviewing this manuscript. I can't thank you enough! Funmi – you ask hard questions – but they serve to push out the best in me. Thank you!

To my sisters of SWM Academy, you know who you are. Thank you!

To my brothers-in-arms, you know who you are. Thank you!

To Tony Hall and the elders of Hope Church, thank you for fostering an environment in which it is possible to grow and thrive.

FOREWORD

Some authors as they put pen to paper adopt a writer's voice, either becoming the teacher and bringing new knowledge to the student or shaping themselves as the examiner, asking life's questions without leading us to fresh understanding. Behind the prose and pictures painted, you never quite feel you have discovered more about them - about their journey, their life and their walk with Jesus.

Emilola Shyllon is not one of those writers.

She does not seek to be autobiographical in her narrative but at the end of this 31-day journey you will be left with the knowledge that you have walked a mile with her along her road of discovery and reflection of what it means to be found in Christ.

The best devotionals do not replace the Christian's daily communion with the Holy Spirit and a desire to spend time praying and to read their Bible. Rather they become a companion who embarks on an exploration alongside of you.

They are sometimes a step ahead, pausing and pointing out a mountain top or vision of majesty that in the rush of our days we can so easily pass by without a second glance. They are sometimes in step with us and bring the voice of encouragement or a whisper of comfort in our ear. The exceptional devotionals do a third thing – which is to be the person standing behind us, pulling back and opening a pathway that allows us to take a few steps of discovery on our own ahead of them. They make a clearing for us to encounter Jesus afresh.

Foreword

Emi is a writer who would wish to be that third companion with us. One who urges us to go even further in our personal relationship with our Saviour. Her passion is for us as readers to grow in our friendship and dependence on Him. Like Peter, in his second letter, Emi is confident Jesus' "divine power has given us everything we need for a godly life through our knowledge of Him who called us by His own glory and goodness".

As you turn the pages of this devotional, allow it to speak to your soul, as it has to mine over the last month and invite the Holy Spirit to bring Jesus clearer into your view.

Tony Hall
Congregational Leader
Hope Church, Orpington

INTRODUCTION

As with all bold sounding claims, there is a backstory. I did not intend to write this devotional at first. I had felt inspired to write a devotional to include poetry a couple of years ago. It was finally published as *Springs of Living Water, a 31-day devotional*. I felt at the end of writing it, that was that! Thank God! I had dispensed with a call laid on my heart. I had seen the dream fulfilled in more ways than I imagined.

I was relieved and although I didn't realise it at the time, a seed for this current devotional was planted in my heart, when I was discussing my plans for Springs of Living Water with a dear brother of mine. He listened patiently as I unpacked my vision. He nodded quietly and said, or rather asked "You do know there's going to be another one after this? You can't expect that this is the only one you will do." I looked at him in stunned silence. Another one? I hadn't thought that far ahead. I mumbled something along the lines of "I don't know, I don't think so." Afterwards, I didn't think any more of his response, apart from to mean a vote of confidence in me.

Fast forward a couple of months later as we raced to the printing of SOLW and beyond. I found myself in deep personal battles as long- standing issues were coming to a head. I was in choppy waters and the only thing keeping me afloat was God. As I poured out my soul in tears, prayers, rants and journaling when I could articulate my emotions, God would send comfort in various ways.

Amid my storms, I sensed the Holy Spirit begin to nudge me that there was, indeed, another devotional. I began to gather

Introduction

my writings – the messages He preached to me in my sorry state. He gave the Word and it was now time to proclaim it. When I finished my first draft and looked over the manuscript, I was surprised to see a theme of hope running through. It seemed to me that what you are about to read is what God intended this devotional to be all along.

The following is a compilation of some of the things He graciously revealed to me during the bleakest of days. Hope became my soul's anchor. In fact, according to Hebrews 6:17-20, that was already and always the case. I was just about to find out, even how much more, this was true.

"In the same way God, desiring even more to show to the heirs of the promise the unchangeableness of His purpose, interposed with an oath, so that by two unchangeable things in which it is impossible for God to lie, we who have taken refuge would have strong encouragement to take hold of the hope set before us. This hope we have as an anchor of the soul, a hope both sure and steadfast and one which enters within the veil, where Jesus has entered as a forerunner for us, having become a high priest forever according to the order of Melchizedek" (Hebrews 6:17-20).

Often in life's choppy waters, our soul bobs about wildly and we fear we will never make it. For those who believe in Christ, we know that we are not alone, yet discouragement nips at our sails and we momentarily forget our sure and steadfast hope, that anchor for the soul.

As depicted in this devotional's cover image, at times the anchor to our boat is not visible. Our hope may appear intangible. Nevertheless, it is there, sure and secure. In preparation for this book, I discovered that anchoring equipment and anchoring techniques are some of the most

Introduction

fundamental aspects of successful sailing. It can be vital to the survival of a boat on the high seas that it is not recommended that you go sailing without mastering the proper use of anchors.

It is therefore my prayer, for every reader, that this devotional will help play its part in reminding us of the strong encouragement to take hold of the hope set before us.

DEDICATION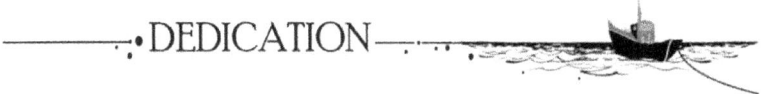

To everyone who has ever had to go through soul-wrenching circumstances.

And to everyone who will.

This is for you.

DAY 1
Don't Give Up!

"Why are you cast down, O my soul? And why are you disquieted within me? Hope in God; for I shall yet praise Him, the help of my countenance and my God." Psalm 43:5 NKJV

Hope is a fragile thing
easily bruised
butterfly wings.
Hope is a tenacious thing
glowing long after
the fire has gone out.
Hope is all you have.
If you lose all
and give out –

Don't ever, ever give up
Hope!

We have all felt it – that precise moment when it seemed all hope is lost! You may even be in that very place right now. The heavens appear overcast and the sun is no longer shining in your world. You feel you will never smile again, let alone laugh. David knew that feeling well. The Psalms are full of him pouring out his heart to God as he counsels himself not to lose hope – to throw whatever was left of his anchor of hope into the stability of God's love and care. If for any reason, your soul is cast down like David, speak to your soul and buoy yourself up by placing your hope (again) in God, who is the help of your countenance. And you will yet praise Him!

Don't Give Up
Thoughts/Prayers

DAY 2
Dealing With Giants

"David said to the Philistine, "You come against me with sword and spear and javelin, but I come against you in the name of the Lord Almighty, the God of the armies of Israel, whom you have defied. This day the Lord will deliver you into my hands, and I'll strike you down and cut off your head. This very day I will give the carcasses of the Philistine army to the birds and the wild animals, and the whole world will know that there is a God in Israel. All those gathered here will know that it is not by sword or spear that the Lord saves; for the battle is the Lord's, and he will give all of you into our hands." As the Philistine moved closer to attack him, David ran quickly toward the battle line to meet him."
1 Samuel 17:45-48 NIV

Do you know how to deal with giants in the land? You don't turn back; you don't keep quiet; you run towards them speaking God's Word. You call to mind what God has done in the past – how He delivered you and gave you victory over the enemy of your soul. That's how you vanquish the enemy! Goliath, the Philistine giant, had been mouthing off all sorts of threats against the armies of Israel which he fully intended to carry out. Forty days and nights he shouted the odds. All of Israel had become greatly afraid and dismayed.

However, the Bible records that through a series of events when David arrived at the battlefield, took sight of Goliath, and heard his threats, something rose on the inside of him. He knew that the God on the inside of him was bigger than the giant before him. In verse 48 of today's text, David ran quickly towards the battle line to meet the Philistine. It was soon over; one of David's smooth stones sank into Goliath's forehead, felling him. David used Goliath's own sword to cut off his head and put a complete end to the giant. In verse 52, the Bible records: "When the Philistines saw that their hero was dead, they turned and ran."

Dealing With Giants

When you deal with giants in your life, the smaller stuff has no choice but to flee! The Lord will give you victory over every giant in your land!

Thoughts/Prayers

DAY 3
Not Without A Struggle

"But My servant Caleb, because he has had a different spirit and has followed Me fully, I will bring into the land which he entered, and his descendants shall take possession of it." Numbers 14:24 NASB

" ...You know the word which the Lord spoke to Moses the man of God concerning you and me in Kadesh-barnea. I was forty years old when Moses the servant of the Lord sent me from Kadesh-barnea to spy out the land, and I brought word back to him as it was in my heart. Nevertheless my brethren who went up with me made the heart of the people melt with fear; but I followed the Lord my God fully. ... Now behold, the Lord has let me live, just as He spoke, these forty-five years, from the time that the Lord spoke this word to Moses, when Israel walked in the wilderness; and now behold, I am eighty-five years old today. I am still as strong today as I was in the day Moses sent me; as my strength was then, so my strength is now, for war and for going out and coming in.

Now then, give me this hill country about which the Lord spoke on that day, for you heard on that day that Anakim were there, with great fortified cities; perhaps the Lord will be with me, and I will drive them out as the Lord has spoken. So Joshua blessed him and gave Hebron to Caleb the son of Jephunneh for an inheritance. Therefore, Hebron became the inheritance of Caleb the son of Jephunneh the Kenizzite until this day, because he followed the Lord God of Israel fully." Joshua 14: 6-15 NASB

When God makes a promise, or gives you a promised land, there will be giants in the land. You may not even know that there are giants in the land until you enter the land but don't let their presence fool or scare you. The land is yours for the taking!

Joshua, Caleb and ten spies entered and saw the promised land. Unfortunately, the ten spies came away with the presence of the giants greater in their minds than the presence of the God who led them into the land. As a result of the children of Israel ignoring the minority report of Joshua and Caleb, they wandered about in the wilderness for forty years! Many died in the process! Yet at the age of eighty-five, forty-five years after Caleb believed the promise and owned the truth that they could take that promised land, he got his promise.

When God makes you a promise, if you hold onto it, He has the power to keep you alive to enjoy that promised thing. You may have to fight to secure the promised land; nevertheless "it" can and will be yours if you choose to believe God over the presence of giants like problems in your life.

Thoughts/Prayers

....

....

....

....

....

....

....

....

DAY 4
"Do It Afraid"

"And the one also who had received the one talent came up and said, 'Master, I knew you to be a hard man... And I was afraid ..." Matthew 25:24-25 NASB

You may have heard the phrase "do it afraid" before. A well-known female Bible teacher coined the phrase "do it afraid". She often tells of the story of a woman who admonished a fearful friend to do it afraid – that which she was afraid of doing – to exemplify taking the steps of faith despite the friend's feelings. The man with one talent in the parable of talents allowed fear to stop him from trying. He was afraid and he concluded that his gift or talent didn't matter, and didn't count in the grand scheme of things, so he buried it. He compared himself to the five-talent guy and the two-talent guy and felt insignificant. He allowed fear to distort the value of his gift and its potential to multiply.

Fear does that – it distorts the truth and sometimes leads to inertia. When the master of the household returned, the man was condemned and damned for not trying at all. He was told that just putting that one talent in the bank would have meant a return on the master's investment. We all feel fear from time to time. It wasn't the feeling of fear that caused the one-talent guy to lose; it was not doing anything in spite of the fear, thinking he had nothing to offer. What did it matter if he buried his gift or talent? After all, the master will still have his one talent back when he returns.

In the movie *"Unconditional"*, Samantha Crawford is happily married and lives on a ranch. The stories she had told and illustrated since childhood have become published books. When her husband is senselessly and tragically killed, Sam loses her faith and will to live. A death-defying encounter with two children unexpectedly leads to a reunion with Joe, her childhood and oldest friend. Joe now cares for and works with children from underprivileged backgrounds. Joe is also suffering from a severe kidney disease and must have dialysis. As Sam watches him live, pray and love the kids, Joe comes to realise that Sam no longer writes. She has given up! With his dying breath, he tells her "Find your stride, Sam, write your story, it matters."

It truly matters what God has placed in you – that dream or idea – no matter how little or insignificant you think it is (which, by the way, is what you feel when you compare your talents to others. This is a No No!). So, whatever your "story" or dream is, please do it, even if it means you have to *do it afraid*, because it matters. Not to have done so, does not even bear thinking about!

Thoughts/Prayers

....

....

....

....

....

....

....

DAY 5
Your Focus

"Looking unto Jesus the author and finisher of our faith..." Hebrews 12:2 KJV

Let us think on the word "author" for a minute. An author is a person who writes a book, an article or document, be it hard or soft copy. A script writer is a person who writes a script for a play, film, or broadcast. A script writer is also therefore an author. He writes the scenes, plots, characters, theme and dialogues. He is in control of the whole landscape of events. Even if the hero or heroine has a few knocks along the way, the author knows how to connect the dots.

He intersperses the events to allow the characters to arrive at the point where he wants them. Now Jesus is the Author of our faith. He gives us a measure of faith at our salvation – faith to believe He is who He says He is. He allows us to be in circumstances which develop our faith. He knows faith is the victory that overcomes the world. 1 John 5:4 NIV. And while we are at it, our faith, whose value is of more worth than gold, is being refined.

Jesus is the finisher of our faith. He is committed to us finishing strong and finishing well no matter what happens to us in the course of our life's events. Jesus told Simon (Peter) as He warned him of his denial in Luke 22:31-32 NIV: "Simon, Simon, Satan has asked to sift all of you as wheat. But I have prayed for you, Simon, that your faith may not fail. And when you have turned back, strengthen your brothers."

Your Focus

You may be sifted as wheat through life's challenges and difficulties, however the Author and Finisher of your faith has prayed for you and is praying for you that your faith will not fail. Be encouraged in your walk of faith today and keep looking unto Jesus.

Thoughts/Prayers

DAY 6
A Precious Ointment, A Costly Worship

"While Jesus was in Bethany in the home of Simon the Leper, a woman came to him with an alabaster jar of very expensive perfume, which she poured on his head as he was reclining at the table. When the disciples saw this, they were indignant. 'Why this waste?' they asked." Matthew 26: 6-8 NIV

This woman, named Mary in John's Gospel account of the story (John 11:2), had an alabaster jar of very costly perfume. She broke it and she worshipped. She worshipped Jesus; she wet His feet with her tears and wiped them with her hair. Some people were dismayed by the way she expressed her worship. Notice the Bible text reads: "when the disciples saw this, they were indignant." They questioned it, they misunderstood it, and they were angered by it.

Notice, the criticism came from the people who were already in the church. Sometimes the people who criticise you or misunderstand you are people who ought to know better! Jesus recognised her worship. Jesus endorsed her worship! And Jesus said because of her actions, many will hear of her. And when they hear of her, her story will point to Jesus. Our worship brings people to Jesus. The Message Bible puts it this way in Romans 12:1 "So here's what I want you to do, God helping you: Take your everyday, ordinary life – your sleeping, eating, going-to-work, and walking-around life – and place it before God as an offering...."

When we live surrendered lives, the aroma of our sacrificial offering is far reaching. My prayer is that whatever represents our alabaster jar of oil will be broken today and every time we appear before God, that many will hear of Him through us.

A Precious Ointment, A Costly Worship

Thoughts/Prayers

DAY 7
I Wonder

"What is man that thou art mindful of him, the son of man that thou takest notice of him?" Psalm 8:4 KJV

I wonder if you know you are beautiful? No, Really!
I wonder if you know the world's a better place
because of you? Yes, Truly!
I wonder if you have any idea that what you do matters,
what you've been through counts? Absolutely!
I wonder if you know you set hearts racing – most of all God's
His thoughts are full of you
I wonder if you'll carry this knowledge with you always
and allow nothing to stop you. Yes, Seriously!

What comes to mind when you hear or see the word 'self-worth'? Underneath your carefully curated image, do you really believe you are worth it? Do you know you are beautiful? Have you got "it's just little old me" mentality that's now an all-consuming thought? Do you think because of age, race, gender, background, social standing or net-worth, that you have nothing meaningful to offer?

Snap out of it! Refuse to drink the devil's cool-aid anymore! God absolutely thinks the world of you! The Psalmist wonders why God thinks so much of man. And he praises God, awestruck at His majesty; considers the splendour of His works and marvels that He made man the crowning glory of everything, the authority and dominion bestowed upon him.

If you ever doubt your worth and His love, among other Scriptures, please call Psalm 8 to mind and remember that you are worth it. He made us and we are the apple of His eye. Never forget it and carry on living your life in the certainty of that!

Thoughts/Prayers

....
....
....
....
....
....
....
....
....
....
....
....
....
....
....
....
....
....

DAY 8
Beyond Redemption?

"Paul, an apostle of Christ Jesus by the will of God ..." Ephesians 1:1 KJV

What a beautiful verse. An amazing record of the redemptive power of God. Grace in action. Paul (then known as Saul) was a terrorist of the early Church. The first time the Bible mentions Saul's name, he was looking after the garments of those who stoned Stephen and was in hearty agreement with their actions. (Acts 7:58, 8:1) That was only the beginning. By verse 3 of Acts 8, he was ravaging the Church, entering home after home, dragging off men and women to be killed. Imagine the children left without parent(s) because of his actions.

Saul made it his life's work to go around killing Christians. So much so, he proceeded to make a road trip out of it (Acts 9:1-6), when an encounter with the Lord brought him to a blinding halt! Saul – accomplice to murder, first degree murderer, and religious leaders' sanctioned killer! – now reads in Ephesians 1:1, "Paul, an apostle of Christ Jesus..."

God alone could make that 180 degree turn of a man's character – to turn an assassin into an evangelist; the addict into a non- addict; the abuser into a totally reformed person; the hateful into the loving; and the one with a wrong purpose into a right calling. There is no one righteous, says the Bible – all have sinned and fall short of the glory of God. (Romans 3:23).

If you are reading this and you have yet to submit your life to God and accept Jesus as your Lord and Saviour, understand your CV may not be as tainted as Paul. Nevertheless, it is still tainted.

Per God's standard it is! And His is the only opinion that matters. Jesus' offer of salvation provides the redemptive grace we all need. If on the other hand, you are already saved and you see your loved ones walking in self-destructive paths, having no regard for God or His ways, be encouraged. If God can do with Paul what He did, then no person you are concerned about is beyond redemption!

Thoughts/Prayers

....
....
....
....
....
....
....
....
....
....
....
....
....
....
....
....

DAY 9
"404 Not Found Error"

"He will again have compassion on us; he will tread our iniquities underfoot. You will cast all our sins into the depths of the sea." Micah 7:19 ESV

When searching for a page on the internet or a web address and you get a "404 not found error" message, it usually means that the page or information you require has been moved or deleted. That in simplistic terms is why you would get an error 404 message. In a similar vein, if you have accepted Christ's sacrifice and His Blood shed for your sins, once your sins are forgiven and cast into the sea, should you go looking for your sins in the sea of His Blood, you won't find them.

What you find is an error message – your sins have been washed away, and they are no longer to be found. They have been buried in the depths of the sea - so deep you can't find them. Isaiah 43:25 states "I, even I, am the one who wipes out your transgression for my own sake. And I will not remember your sins." Now, a number of tools exist that can trawl through websites to find pages which return a 404-error message. However, in respect of your sins, once brought to Jesus, they are swallowed up by His blood.

God gives His promise in Hebrews 8:12 to forgive and not remember your sins. So, just so you know, Jesus' blood has deleted your sins and has moved them as far as the east is from the west. Instead of searching for your sins just because you don't "feel forgiven", rather let your soul bless the Lord (Psalms 103) and thank Him for His many benefits, one of which includes removing all your sins and not remembering them again.

404 Not Found Error

Thoughts/Prayers

DAY 10
Counted Joy, Considered Joy

"Consider it pure joy, my brothers and sisters, whenever you face trials of many kinds, because you know that the testing of your faith produces perseverance." James 1: 2-3 NIV

Remember that well known song "Count your blessings, name them one by one. Count your blessings, see what God has done! Count your blessings, name them one by one. And it will surprise you what the Lord has done." Now I'm not speaking of counting your obvious blessings. Those are not a chore to count at all. I'm speaking of those times when the illness hasn't gone away; the infertility is still staring you in the face; the marriage has spluttered to a stop; a child is still off the rails; and the finances, *what finances*?

Consider it an opportunity for joy, James said. He is not speaking of a Pollyanna syndrome here but the opportunity for us to become more Christ-like and spiritually mature as we go through hard places. It is said that under pressure you know what you believe and you believe what you know. It is by no means easy to count it all joy. In fact, joy is the last thing that springs to mind when I'm in such places. But the very things that test our faith produce perseverance. "Let perseverance finish its work so that you may be mature and complete, not lacking anything" James 1:4 NIV.

Thoughts/Prayers

DAY 11
Seven Times Hotter (1)

"...He answered by giving orders to heat the furnace seven times more than it was usually heated. He commanded certain valiant warriors who were in his army to tie up Shadrach, Meshach and Abed-nego, in order to cast them into the furnace of blazing fire. Then these men were tied up in their trousers, their coats, their caps and their other clothes, and were cast into the midst of the furnace of blazing fire. For this reason, because the king's command was urgent and the furnace had been made extremely hot, the flame of the fire slew those men who carried up Shadrach, Meshach and Abed-nego. But these three men, Shadrach, Meshach and Abed-nego, fell into the midst of the furnace of blazing fire still tied up." Daniel 3: 19-22 NASB

Shadrach, Meshach and Abed-nego had refused to bow down to worship the golden idol made on the order of King Nebuchadnezzar even though it was a government decree. To ignore this edict meant certain death! When Nebuchadnezzar became aware of these Jewish men's stance, he became enraged. Daniel's mates were thrown into the furnace made seven times hotter for them. However, this heathen king's wicked move set the stage for us to learn a few things:

(1) The presence of the Lord in their predicament was a cooling agent. In Acts 17:28 NASB, the Bible says "for in Him we live and move and exist ......", so whatever comes to us has to come through Him first! They lived, they moved and had their being in Him, in the midst of what was meant to consume them. What are you going through that is seven times hotter? What predicament has overwhelmed you that has got the signature of the devil all over it? Behold the Son of God is in it with you!

(2) *Jesus spoke with the men – the Lord will speak with you!* In verse 24 -25 Nebuchadnezzar was stunned to see four men loosed and walking about in the fire. "...Was it not three men we cast bound into the midst of the fire?" They replied to the king, "Certainly, O king." He said, "Look! I see four men loosed and walking about in the midst of the fire, without harm, and the appearance of the fourth is like a son of the gods!" And we may safely assume that if the fourth one who had a godly appearance was walking around with the men, He would have been talking with them too! The Lord will give you specific and divine revelations while you are going through fire. "Call on me in the day of trouble and I will answer you." (Psalm 50:15)

Thoughts/Prayers

....
....
....
....
....
....
....
....
....
....
....

DAY 12
Seven Times Hotter (2)

"Then Nebuchadnezzar came near to the door of the furnace of blazing fire; he responded and said, "Shadrach, Meshach and Abed-nego, come out, you servants of the Most High God, and come here!" Then Shadrach, Meshach and Abed-nego came out of the midst of the fire." "...and saw in regard to these men that the fire had no effect on the bodies of these men nor was the hair of their head singed, nor were their trousers damaged, nor had the smell of fire even come upon them." "Nebuchadnezzar responded and said, "Blessed be the God of Shadrach, Meshach and Abed-nego, who has sent His angel and delivered His servants who put their trust in Him, violating the king's command, and yielded up their bodies so as not to serve or worship any god except their own God... Then the king caused Shadrach, Meshach and Abed- nego to prosper in the province of Babylon." Daniel 3:26 -30 NASB

(3) *Whatever is designed to annihilate or consume you now has the opposite effect.* In fact, there will be no evidence that you went through the fire. The stench, the smoke, the singed hair and the charred effects of being in a fire – none were to be found on these children of Israel. The ropes that were used to bind them, such that they fell into the blazing fire still tied up, were eaten up by the fire. Seeing the previously bound men loosed and walking about with a fourth man astounded the heathen king Nebuchadnezzar.

In the name of Jesus, those things which limited your progress and restricted your movements like the ropes, shall be consumed in whatever furnace of affliction you have found yourself! The Lord will use the 7-times-hotter-situation to consume everything that He has not planted in your life. You are not only coming out – you are coming out promoted!

(4) *They came out of the blazing situation.* Once the King of kings has intervened in a matter, earthly kings have no other course of action but to follow a divine mandate! And then Nebuchadnezzar uttered his own praise and recognition of God's power. He also made a decree of grievous judgement against anyone who said anything offensive against the God of Shadrach, Meshach and Abed-nego, whilst not forgetting to see to the prosperity of these men in the Babylonian kingdom.

Thoughts/Prayers

DAY 13
My Scars, Your Proof

"The righteous will flourish like a palm tree......" Psalm 92:12 NIV

A palm tree is said to be one of the most useful trees on earth. The uses include edible staples, drink, flooring, furniture, building materials, animal fodder, medicines, boat construction, oil, wax and many, many more. There are hundreds and hundreds of uses. Just as every part of a palm tree is useful in one form or the other, so everything in the life of a child of God is useful for God's glory. The pleasant and not so pleasant parts of that life. Do not dismiss the value of anything you have been through – nothing is wasted in Christ.

It is interesting to note that in some species of the palm tree, when the tree loses its leaves at the bottom of the canopy, new ones grow from the top of the canopy. The tree trunk elongates as a result. The portion of the stem located below the canopy is typically covered in round scars from where the leaves were attached. On some palm trees, these scars form circular ridges which make the tree easier to climb. The scars then turn to small hand and footholds for a climber to go up and down the tree. Thus again, showcasing our God's intention that everything, even a palm tree's scar, has its uses.

In response to Thomas doubting the reality of a risen Christ, Jesus said to him in John 20:27 "......Reach here with your finger, and see My hands; and reach here your hand and put it into My side; and do not be unbelieving, but believing." Jesus showed Thomas His scars and invited him to start believing and cease doubting. "God is able to make all things work together for good" is a well-known scripture. He can make (use) all things — even the scars of what you have been through - as a testimony that God is alive and He is able to bring others out. Just as He brought you out of that situation you went through! Although Jesus commends those who believed without seeing, there will be some people who will not believe until they see the scars. Choose rather to be the one whose scars tell of the Saviour's redemption and God's deliverance rather than the one asking to see evidence of it!

Thoughts/Prayers

....
....
....
....
....
....
....
....
....
....
....
....
....
....

DAY 14
He Calls You By Name

"But now, this is what the Lord, your Creator says, O Jacob, And He who formed you, O Israel, "Do not fear, for I have redeemed you [from captivity]; I have called you by name; you are Mine!" Isaiah 43:1 AMP

They called her the woman
with the issue of blood;
Jesus called her daughter.
He was called a paralytic man
but Jesus called him son.
Your circumstances may have
renamed you – barren, infertile,
unemployed, terminally ill,
divorced, single, lonely,
poor and the list is endless.
You may not have even heard
anyone call your name
in a loving way, in a long time.
Today hear Jesus calling
your name.
He calls you daughter.
He calls you son.
Allow Him to give you
an identity makeover.
He loves you – you are precious to Him.
Hear Him call your name;
He longs to make you whole.

He Calls You By Name

Let today's reading cause you to pause and thank Him that He calls you by name. You are not what you are going through. You are no longer a slave; you are a child of God. And God never forsakes His child.

Thoughts/Prayers

DAY 15
How To Dress For Victory (1)

"Therefore, put on the full armour of God so that when the evil day comes, you may be able to stand your ground." Ephesians 6:11 NIV

Therefore, put on the full armour of God so that when, not if, the evil day comes, you may be able to stand your ground. Evil days are a surety! Jesus speaks of us having trouble in the world. Job 5:7 NIV speaks of man being born to trouble as surely as sparks fly upward. The Bible recommends the full armour of God as an answer to the evil day.

(1) The belt of truth buckled around your waist. It is fitting that the belt of truth is the first piece of the whole armour of God. It is the first part of the armour listed because, without truth, we are lost, and the schemes of the devil will surely overpower us. Jesus is the way, the truth, and the life and we only come to God through Him (John 14:6). Without truth, the rest of the armour would be of no use to us. You cannot know who you really are, and who you are truly made to be, apart from God! That is the Truth embodied in Jesus Christ!

A belt was often worn as part of the Roman Legion military outfit, to help hold the sword and other weapons. The belt of a Roman soldier in Paul's day was not a simple leather strap such as we wear today. It was a thick, heavy leather and metal band with protective strips hanging down the front of it. The belt of truth protects us and prepares us for the battle that is part of every Christian's life.

(2) A breastplate of righteousness to defend you. A breastplate acts as a barrier or protection between your chest, where your heart resides, and the object or weapon intended to cause you harm. Righteousness is right standing with God. The Bible says, "above all else, guard your heart, for everything you do flows from it" (Proverbs 4:23). Righteousness is defence. "No weapon formed against you shall prosper, and every tongue which rises against you in judgment, you shall condemn. This is the heritage of the servants of the LORD, and their righteousness is from me." (Isaiah 54:17). If our heart is poisoned, and out of the heart come the issues of life, then it will poison the rest of our life (relationships, finances, mental attitude).

(3) Your feet shod with the readiness that comes from the gospel of peace. Be an example of the Word wherever your feet go in the course of your day. We are made ready by the gospel of peace, not our strength. "And how shall they preach, except they be sent? As it is written, How beautiful are the feet of them that preach the gospel of peace, and bring glad tidings of good things" (Romans 10:15). Ask yourself, are you dressed for victory today?

Thoughts/Prayers

....

....

....

....

....

DAY 16
How To Dress For Victory (2)

"Wherefore take unto you the whole armour of God, that ye may be able to withstand in the evil day, and having done all, to stand." Ephesians 6:13 KJV

In continuation from yesterday's subject, let us consider the following:

(4) In addition to all these (not an optional requirement) take up the shield of faith to extinguish all the flaming arrows of the evil one. A shield of faith to protect and defend. In medieval battles, flaming arrows were used by fighting armies to cause maximum hurt. An arrow, which was already a deadly weapon with a sharpened, often poisoned tip, was dipped in tar and set alight. It was then launched into its target. The arrows were not designed just to hurt, but to kill – apart from the victim being felled by an arrow now lodged in his body, he was then burning up at the same time. We may not notice any flaming arrows physically today but Satan's devices are still as deadly.

(5) Take the helmet of salvation. A helmet is designed to protect the head of the wearer; to protect his life in battle. God's salvation plan through Jesus is the only way we can make it through this life to the next.

Put on the helmet of salvation and (6) the sword of the Spirit which is the Word of God. A sword is made to wound or kill. Its tip, length and sharpness all designed for one purpose in mind – to be of use in the holder's hands (when used properly) to deliver the desired outcome. Isaiah 55:11 ESV "So shall my word be that goes out from my mouth; it will not return to me empty, but it shall accomplish that which I purpose, and shall succeed in the thing for which I sent it." The sword of the Spirit is our only offensive weapon. It is the only thing effective in knocking the devil down flat and sending him running every time.

In Hebrews 4:12, the Word of God is described as a two-edged sword. It is double- edged, so whichever way you swing it, the Word is effective. Whether in your marriage or at work, over your relationships or your earning power, over sickness and all sorts of phobias and addiction and everything the devil slings at you. The Word of God is capable of slaying everything which exalts itself against the knowledge of Christ. The Christian life is a battle! It is warfare on a grand scale.

Put on the whole armour *of God,* not an armour of your own making, not of money, skill or beauty. Not someone else but of God. Notice amongst the articles of armour, there is no protection for your back, that's because God's got your back! (2 Timothy 2:3-4). You are enlisted. It's your duty to take up the battle cry and do battle. When you resist the devil in God's strength, he will flee from you.

Thoughts/Prayers

....
....
....
....
....

DAY 17
The Lord's Battle

"A lion has roared! Who will not fear? The Lord God has spoken! Who can but prophesy?" Amos 3:8 NASB

"This is what the Lord says to me: As a lion growls, a great lion over its prey—and though a whole band of shepherds is called together against it, it is not frightened by their shouts or disturbed by their clamour—so the Lord Almighty will come down to do battle on Mount Zion and on its heights." Isaiah 31:4 NIV

The Lord will go to great lengths to rescue and deliver, whether the situation you find yourself in is self-inflicted or you are being oppressed by some other person(s); even if Satan is busy pointing out that because of your actions and poor decisions, you deserve to be under his management, the way the animals cowered over belong to the shepherd. However, as a lion is not fazed by a band of shepherds coming against it as it growls over its prey, so the Lord is not fazed by anything or anyone protesting that you rightfully belong to them. He has come down to Mount Zion to do battle for you.

You are His and just as nothing can snatch the prey from the lion's hold, nothing can snatch you out of His hand. No matter the shouts or clamour of the devil as he disputes God's right to have you – pointing out that you are a sinner or you still live in secret sin – the Lord has come to do battle for you! He is delivering the lawful captives. Hear the roar of the Lion of Judah in your spirit setting you free and reminding you who really is King and in control.

The Lord's Battle
Thoughts/Prayers

DAY 18
Trading Places

"Come to Me, all who are weary and heavy-laden, and I will give you rest. Take My yoke upon you and learn from Me, for I am gentle and humble in heart, and you will find rest for your souls." Matthew 11:28-29 NASB

You've heard the song
I'm trading my sorrows
I'm trading my shame
I'm laying it down
For the joy of the Lord
The cross of Jesus
Is our trading place.
It's where we are invited
To trade our sin for His salvation
Grief and sorrow for His joy
Our guilt and shame for
His pardon and peace
His blood legalises the exchange
It guarantees us in this life
Through to the next
Have you got things, you
Need to trade off?
Come to Jesus, come to the Cross
There awaits the best trade off you will ever make.

Are you burdened today? Is there something weighing on your mind? Whether it is guilt or shame-inducing, fear-eliciting, however major or minor. Whether you have been a Christian for 30 years or 30 minutes, Jesus invites you to come to Him and trade your heavy burdens for His. If you are yet to place your trust in the Lord, and to believe on His name, today is the day of salvation. Do not ignore the gentle tugging felt in your heart. (At the back of this devotional there is a prayer you can say, otherwise called the Sinner's prayer.) Pause in your day and pray where you are. Thank Him for this divine exchange and believe that it is done.

Thoughts/Prayers

DAY 19
Heart Conditions

"Let not your hearts be troubled. Believe in God; believe also in me." John 14:1 ESV

Do you know the best antidote for troubled hearts, bruised hearts or broken hearts? When waves of pain wash over you and you feel your heart is one mass of pulsating agony. Jesus said in John 16:33 NIV: "I have told you these things, so that in me you may have peace. In this world you will have trouble. But take heart! I have overcome the world." We have all felt what it means for our hearts to be troubled.

Job 5: 7 KJV states: "Yet man is born to trouble as surely as sparks fly upward." However, the antidote to trouble is to believe in God, believe in Jesus, and believe in His words. He has said in Him you will have peace. There may be trouble all around *but in Him* you will have peace! And we know that "…the peace of God, which transcends all understanding, will guard your hearts and your minds…" Philippians 4:7 NIV. So, when next your heart is in a state, remember to take the antidote!

Heart Conditions
Thoughts/Prayers

DAY 20
Lessons From Lazarus

"It is the Spirit who gives life, the flesh profits for nothing. The words that I have spoken to you they are Spirit and life." John 6:63 NASB

Jesus said to Lazarus "come forth" John 11:43 KJV. (1) *He sent His word and His word raised the dead man.* "He sent out His word and healed them; He rescued them from the grave" Psalm 107:20 NIV. Jesus cried out with a loud voice. It was a serious situation! You don't cry out unless something is at stake. Whether your cry is in delight or not, no adult cries out just because! Jesus sent His word and His word brought out Lazarus. The Word of God is a messenger; a servant who obeys His master in what it has been sent to do. It is a productive and effective servant. So, dear reader, deploy the Word of God in your life!

(2) *Jesus said to them roll away (or take away in some versions) the stone.* Jesus could have waved His hand and the stone would have moved away. He could have gotten angels to move away the stone; however, He did not, because there are some things you need to do by yourself.

What He has given you the ability or power to do for yourself, He won't do for you. You will need to fill in that application for that job interview, start exercising and living well, budget and keep within your financial perimeters, actively pursue that business idea or create or maintain a peaceful atmosphere in your home. Oh yes, He gives strength to the weary and His word will make the impossible possible, but you still need to act on what you can!

(3) *At times, the only action you can take is getting your mouth to be His mouthpiece.* Speak His words over that situation; send out your words (being His Word) and cause that person or situation to be rescued out of the grave – be it unemployment, financial worries, childlessness, depression, ill health, you name it! And just as Jesus raised Lazarus and told them loose him and let him go, the grave clothes which bound him were loosed, his limbs were loosed, his mouth was loosed, and every part of him created for movement was loosed and set free, so too will the Spirit who gives life bring about a change of location in every area of your life where you have or are experiencing loss in Jesus' name.

Thoughts/Prayers

....

....

....

....

....

....

....

....

....

....

....

....

DAY 21
Transition

"Do not despise these small beginnings, for the Lord rejoices to see the work begin …." Zechariah 4:10 NLT

Colour me Spring
brushstrokes of Grace
turning the dark places
of my life,
into starting points
of Destiny.
Skilful hands, going
over a muted canvas
bring alive the changes
I seek.
Colour me Spring.
Colour me beautiful.

Quite often the place where we are bears no resemblance to the place we are going. Similar to many heroes of faith in the Bible, we may have a word from the Lord in one or several areas of our lives. However, our current experience is anything but the word in reality. Keep holding on. God specialises in turning dark places into defining moments of destiny. Joseph, faithfully running the prison administration, perhaps not without occasionally reminiscing, had no idea he would one day be running the whole economy of his captive country!

Ruth, Naomi's daughter-in-law was widowed, childless and landless. By the time God's brushstrokes of grace settled on the canvas of her life, she was remarried and fruitful, no longer poor and firmly written into the lineage of Jesus Christ! Do not despise the day of small beginnings (or even transition periods). God always has an end in view far bigger than what we can contemplate.

Thoughts/Prayers

DAY 22
It Runs In The Family

"But as many as received Him, to them He gave the right to become children of God, even to those who believe in His name." John 1:12 NASB

"It runs in the family", "it runs in my family". Many times, when we hear those comments, it's usually because a negative trait or disease is being talked about. Of course, it may also mean an academic genius, business acumen, financial prowess or spiritual heritage. The list of positive things is endless. However, often than not, it's the negative traits which run in a family that are being highlighted.

May I bring to your remembrance other things – much more important things – that run in your family because you are of God's family. 2 Corinthians 5:17 NASB "Therefore if anyone is in Christ, he is a new creature; the old things passed away; behold, new things have come." As a result of this new connection, forgiveness runs in your family (Colossians 3:13); perseverance, self-discipline runs in your family (1 Peter 1:3-8); love runs in your family (2 Timothy 1:7). We have not been given a spirit of fear but of love, power and of a sound mind. Hope and a positive outlook runs in your family (Proverbs 23:18).

I could go on and on, but you get the picture. Now go live your life in the knowledge of all these great and magnificent attributes which run in your family.

Thoughts/Prayers

DAY 23
A Reminder

"But Zion said, The Lord hath forsaken me, and my Lord hath forgotten me. Can a woman forget her sucking child, that she should not have compassion on the son of her womb? Yea, they may forget, yet will I not forget thee." Isaiah 49:14-15 KJV

You catch my tears
in your hands.
My soul hunkers
down in you.
I have come to
the end of me,
and I look to you
for sustenance;
You remind me,
"I never left,
your tears do not fall
to the ground in vain.
You are precious to me,
and I love you.
I have loved you
before you were born
and every second since."

In your troubled moments today, be reminded of God's love and His promises. He has promised not to forget you or anything which concerns you. If you are in a place where your heart's song is like Zion's in Isaiah 49:14 – the Lord has forsaken me, and my God has forgotten me – be reminded that He really cares. Be encouraged for He truly loves you. Pray this prayer with me: Father, let your love penetrate my heart. Let me become more aware of your presence. Let me know and sense your love. Let the certainty of it keep me buoyed in life's circumstances, in Jesus' name. Amen

Thoughts/Prayers

DAY 24
"E For Effort Not Excuses"

"Then the man who had received one bag of gold came. 'Master,' he said, 'I knew that you are a hard man, harvesting where you have not sown and gathering where you have not scattered seed. So I was afraid and went out and hid your gold in the ground. See, here is what belongs to you." Matthew 25:24-25 NIV

Years ago, at a church seminar, I heard a man who is now of blessed memory make the statement "E for Effort, not Excuses" and it struck a chord. When the Lord first breathed the idea of a part devotional, part poetry book into my spirit, I immediately thought of some reasons why I couldn't do it now – no money, little time and energy. Besides, what did I have to write?

Then I heard Him ask simply "Yes, why not?" Then, I pondered 'yes, why not?' as I knelt in my bedroom. I had just started to pray for direction – I felt I was made for more. But I didn't know what exactly more meant. As His still small voice spoke amidst the clamouring of my heart and then I said yes, I immediately felt peace.

I felt full of peace and clarity as the lingering confusion faded away. It felt like the quickest answer to prayer I had ever received. Once I stopped making excuses, the resources came, help came. I received a phone call which led to a series of events which helped clear the way. One of the results of my E for Effort is the book you are now reading from. When next you consider the talents God has given you, like the man in the Parable of Talents, remember E for Effort, not Excuses!

"E For Effort not Excuses"

Thoughts/Prayers

DAY 25
Your Welfare Package

"For I know the plans I have for you," declares the Lord, "plans to prosper you and not to harm you, plans to give you hope and a future." Jeremiah 29:11 NIV

On a train station platform while waiting for a train, I was watching building work and regeneration of the area around me. I stood watching as a forklift began its process of moving objects. It was a mini forklift. And then I felt the Holy Spirit say look at the forked hands of the machine coming at the object to be transported. He then said, "The things I allow to come towards you are not to destroy you but they are to lift you up. It is not to destroy you but ultimately to lift you up."

A forklift's arm, for example, goes into a bale of hay but it is not to destroy or scatter that bale of hay but to lift it from one area to another place – where it will be used. Notice that Scripture reads "...to prosper you and not to harm you...to give you..." It's all been designed with you in mind. There is no haphazard, afterthought, cut and paste approach to this plan. And no one knows these plans like the Lord. He has the blueprint of your future in hand. Let this promise cause your heart to find its rest anew in God today.

Your Welfare Package

Thoughts/Prayers

DAY 26
Made To Prosper, Made For More

"But the Lord was with Joseph and extended kindness to him, and gave him favor in the sight of the chief jailer. The chief jailer committed to Joseph's charge all the prisoners who were in the jail; so that whatever was done there, he was responsible for it. The chief jailer did not supervise anything under Joseph's charge because the Lord was with him; and whatever he did, the Lord made to prosper." Genesis 39: 21-23 NASB

Joseph was in charge of the prison. The favour of God was upon him yet after interpreting the cup bearer's dream in Genesis 40: 14, Joseph said to the cup bearer, "But when all goes well with you, remember me and show me kindness; mention me to Pharaoh and get me out of this prison." He had it good in prison considering his circumstances. There was no doubt about that, but prison was not home. It was still a prison at the best of times!

Joseph had been in charge at Potiphar's house and also while imprisoned but he knew he was made for more. Notwithstanding the current favour and success plus the Lord's presence which he enjoyed, he felt - and rightly so - that this was not the end. God had given him dreams of his future. And even though Joseph had no idea that the path to his future contained a stint in prison, he knew his current situation was not final. He expressed his dissatisfaction with his continued imprisonment.

Perhaps you are in a situation where although you are experiencing God's blessings in certain areas of your life, one area has you locked down in pain or prison. It may even be that things are going so well, people say you have it good, but you know deep inside of you – God has made you for more! I call this a holy dissatisfaction. Don't settle for the status quo however pleasant. Reach out, nay, cry out for all that God has purposed for you. While Joseph was in Potiphar's house, he may have thought his dreams would happen through him rising through the ranks. But by the time he landed in prison, he knew without a doubt that this was not meant to be his permanent address. The journey from pit to palace may be protracted. Joseph had been in prison for quite a while, and a full two years passed after the cup bearer's dream interpretation before Joseph was remembered. Imagine his pain amid the apparent blessings in the prison.

But God, who has the times and seasons in His hands, caused the cup bearer's amnesia to lift at the right time. Things were set in motion for Joseph to walk into all that God had revealed and prepared for him. That day, upon answering Pharaoh's summons, Joseph's dissatisfaction was assuaged. Bottom line: don't settle for less than God has in mind for you! No matter how pleasant things seem at present in life, work or ministry, that holy dissatisfaction deep in your spirit is often a signal that you are made for more.

Thoughts/Prayers

....
....
....
....
....
....

DAY 27
Prison Mates

"Set me free from my prison, that I may praise your name. Then the righteous will gather about me because of your goodness to me."
Psalm 142:7 NASB

Your stretch in prison can be determined by the one you are in prison with. Pharaoh had put his chief cup bearer and chief baker in prison for offending him. We are not told what the offence was but it was enough to land them in Egypt's gulag. They ended up in the same prison in which Joseph was incarcerated. At the time they were imprisoned, they had no idea how fortunate they would be for that fact – at least for the cup bearer. Neither did Joseph realise how instrumental the cup bearer would be to his release date at the time (Genesis 40:1-4).

According to Acts 16 verses 25-26, Paul and Silas had been imprisoned for delivering a fortune teller. Her owners, bereft at the loss of earnings and future income, caused them to be dragged before the authorities who had Paul and Silas thrown in prison. However, midnight found Paul and Silas praying and singing hymns to God, and the other prisoners were listening. A violent earthquake followed, shaking the prison foundations. Prison doors flew open and everyone's chains came loose!

In Luke 4 verses 18 -21 NIV Jesus reading in the temple quoted Isaiah 61 verses 1-3 "the Spirit of the Lord is on me, because the He has anointed me …to proclaim freedom for the prisoners and … to set the oppressed free…. After reading, Jesus closed the book, gave it back to the attendants and sat down. "Today this Scripture is fulfilled in your hearing."

Not everyone reading this will have had an inside knowledge of being in a prison, but we can all be imprisoned in one form or another by different degrees of pain and problems. Can I implore you to invite Jesus into your prison? He is the One who has the power to deliver all who are oppressed by the devil. He is the only one who executes justice for the oppressed. Psalm 146:7 NASB "...The Lord sets the prisoners free."

Thoughts/Prayers

DAY 28
Lessons From A Boat (1)

"Immediately He made the disciples get into the boat and go ahead of Him to the other side, while He sent the crowds away. ...But the boat was already a long distance from the land, battered by the waves; for the wind was contrary. And in the fourth watch of the night He came to them, walking on the sea." Matthew 14:22, 24-25 NASB

Jesus had just finished the miracle of feeding the five thousand. The disciples were on assignment. They were on a journey sanctioned by God and had been given a clear directive. 'Get into the boat and go ahead of me to the other side.' And the disciples did so. There are some lessons to be learned from this text.

(1) *Sometimes when you are on a journey commissioned by God, trouble may arise.* Verse 24 reads "But the boat was already a long distance from the land, battered by the waves; for the wind was contrary." There was no doubt about it, despite Jesus' clear instructions, opposition arose, and negative forces appeared to prevail. That should help remind us that if we have a clear word from the Lord, that will not preclude us from trouble.

The boat was already a long distance from the land. (2)*Thank God! We have a God who goes the distance.* When the prodigal son was a long distance away, the father saw him and ran towards him (Luke 15:20). Matthew 14:25 reads "and in the fourth watch of the night He came to them, walking on the sea". Jesus walked towards the disciples' situation – he walked into it. Although they were a distance away from their goal, Jesus came to where they were to help them. No matter how far away you are from where you need to be, or however far away from the Father's heart and embrace, He will make the distance to help you.

Thoughts/Prayers

DAY 29
Lessons From A Boat (2)

"When the disciples saw Him walking on the sea, they were terrified, and said, "It is a ghost!" And they cried out in fear. But immediately Jesus spoke to them, saying, "Take courage, it is I; do not be afraid." Peter said to Him, "Lord, if it is You, command me to come to You on the water." And He said, "Come!" And Peter got out of the boat, and walked on the water and came toward Jesus. But seeing the wind, he became frightened, and beginning to sink, he cried out, "Lord, save me!" Immediately Jesus stretched out His hand and took hold of him, and said to him, "You of little faith, why did you doubt?" When they got into the boat, the wind stopped." Matthew 14:26-32 NASB

(3) *Perception is everything.* Verse 26: As a result of what the disciples saw and how they interpreted what they saw, they were afraid and cried out "it is a ghost!" even though they were witnessing one of the greatest recorded miracles – Jesus walking on water (not walking on dry land through water as their ancestors did at the Red Sea, but on the Sea!)

Fear will make you misinterpret situations; respond negatively to what should be celebrated. It will affect your perception and pollute your confession. That was why Jesus immediately spoke to them correcting their perception and interpretation of what they saw. "Take courage, it is I, don't be afraid." Peter, inspired to faith by Jesus' command, said in effect, if it's really you Jesus, tell me to come. Jesus simply replied "Come." Peter obeyed and started to walk on water as Jesus did. Then he saw the wind, his perception of the situation altered, fear entered him and he began to sink. He began to be overwhelmed by the very thing that he was on top of just a moment ago.

Lessons From a Boat (2)

(4) Notice that the contrary wind did not stop until they got into the boat. When Jesus was walking on water, the winds were there. When Peter obeyed the command to come walking, the winds were still there. Peter "saw" the winds instead of Jesus who stood before him. When he perceived the negative winds instead of keeping his gaze and focus on Jesus, he started to sink. In everything and in all areas of life, God's perspective is the most important thing. Faith is God's perspective!

As and when His purposes and plans are revealed to you (Ephesians 2:10), there will be opposition to you obeying His commands. However, fear not, and keep your gaze on Jesus. Listen only for His voice and not the baying voice of the contrary winds. Ask for and keep God's perspective when viewing your life with its twists and turns. He who has called you is faithful. He will lead you safely to shore.

Thoughts/Prayers

DAY 30
The Main Thing

"One of the criminals who were hanged there was hurling abuse at Him, saying, "Are You not the Christ? Save Yourself and us!" But the other answered, and rebuking him said, "Do you not even fear God, since you are under the same sentence of condemnation? And we indeed are suffering justly, for we are receiving what we deserve for our deeds; but this man has done nothing wrong." And he was saying, "Jesus, remember me when You come in Your kingdom!" And He said to him, "Truly I say to you, today you shall be with Me in Paradise." Luke 23:39-43 NASB

Ever wondered how or why Jesus did not collapse under the sheer weight of the need and demands of people around Him? Legitimate needs and demands, such as healing, deliverance, provision and salvation and the like. The sick, hungry, blind, deaf and dumb regularly surrounded Him. There is only so much that can be done in a day, even by Jesus! It was simple, Jesus knew and understood His purpose (John 10:10).

He had a clear and strong understanding of who God sent Him to. He did not respond to every need around Him. He did not allow the thief on the left hand to guilt trip Him, as the need for deliverance was pointed out. He gave no indication that He had even heard what that thief said. He however responded to faith. As the thief on the right hand uttered his rebuke and made a plea, Jesus responded straightaway! He who came to save those who were lost and had put their faith in Him, met the dying criminal at the point of his need.

The Bible says wisdom is the principal thing and in all thy getting, get understanding. An understanding of your

The Main Thing

purpose or – put this way – God's purpose for your life, will set you free from unending demands of people. This year, ask for wisdom to find and to know your purpose. This will keep you doing the Father's bidding, not yours or the ones laid on you by others. Ask every day for grace and strength to ignore what truly does not speak into that purpose.

Thoughts/Prayers

....
....
....
....
....
....
....
....
....
....
....
....
....
....

DAY 31
My Life, A Contradiction?

"And the people stood by, looking on. And even the rulers were sneering at Him, saying, "He saved others; let Him save Himself if this is the Christ of God, His Chosen One." The soldiers also mocked Him, coming up to Him, offering Him sour wine, and saying, "If You are the King of the Jews, save Yourself!" Luke 23:35-37 NASB

Jesus hung on the cross, dying, yet He had declared He came to save. Often there are times, seasons or situations in your life which appear contradictory to your purpose, calling or belief. You preach the Word to others but members of your household are not interested. You take care of other people's children while your arms ache to hold your own. In obedience, you gave your last dime but you don't know how you are going to pay for your family's needs. Your counselling helps other people's marriages while yours is floundering!

Bruised and hanging on the cross that Friday afternoon on Golgotha, Jesus' life and ministry seemed to be one huge contradiction. But what the enemy doesn't know, what people failed to see, is that it is that very thing God is going to use to announce that He is God over your life.

That seemingly contradictory state of affairs contains the ingredients of your ministry, the elements of your transformation to the next level. In Luke 23:39, one of the criminals who hung on a cross alongside Jesus, hurled abuse at him. "Are you not the Christ, save yourself and us." Your office is to save and here you are hanging and dying on a cross. While you are going through that horrible place, the devil is hurling discouragement, doubt and fear at you. People are mocking, snickering behind your back and some, like the criminal on the left, even say it to your face! Didn't you say you were a Christian, why is such and such happening to you?

But it's only Friday! Sunday is coming. Just as the devil and the naysayers didn't know back then, the Resurrection is coming. That major hiccup is about to become God's slam-dunk! Soon the God of peace will crush the enemy under your feet.

Let the response of the criminal on the right side of Jesus inspire you today. He recognised that this grievous spectacle before him was nothing less than God's grand salvation plan in verses 40-43. The thing that the enemy meant for evil in your life or the lives of your loved ones is God's template for a glorious end!

Thoughts/Prayers

Sinner's Prayer

Lord Jesus, I repent of my sins, come into my heart and have your way, I make you my Lord and Saviour. Amen (Romans 10:9)

If you prayed this simple prayer, I believe you got born again. Do join a good Bible-based church and give Jesus first place in your life. God is rooting for you!

www.ingramcontent.com/pod-product-compliance
Lightning Source LLC
Chambersburg PA
CBHW060420050426
42449CB00009B/2046